Free Verse Editions

Edited by Jon Thompson

THE CURIOSITIES

Brittany Perham

Parlor Press
Anderson, South Carolina
www.parlorpress.com

Parlor Press LLC, Anderson, South Carolina, 29621

© 2012 by Parlor Press
Printed in the United States of America
S A N: 2 5 4 - 8 8 7 9

Library of Congress Cataloging-in-Publication Data

Perham, Brittany, 1981-
  The curiosities / Brittany Perham.
      p. cm. -- (Free verse editions)
   ISBN 978-1-60235-239-1 (pbk. : acid-free paper) -- ISBN 978-
1-60235-240-7 (adobe ebook)
   I. Title.
   PS3616.E744C87 2012
   811'.6--dc23
                                    2011042922

Cover design by David Blakesley.
Cover image: "Ruth" by Carla Shapiro. Platinum/palladium print
on handmade rice paper, gampi. © 2007 by Carla Shapiro. Used
by permission.

Printed on acid-free paper.

Parlor Press, LLC is an independent publisher of scholarly and
trade titles in print and multimedia formats. This book is available
in paperback and ebook formats from Parlor Press on the World
Wide Web at http://www.parlorpress.com or through online and
brick-and-mortar bookstores. For submission information or to
find out about Parlor Press publications, write to Parlor Press,
3015 Brackenberry Drive, Anderson, South Carolina, 29621, or
e-mail editor@parlorpress.com.

For C.J.

Contents

3

THE CURIOSITIES

1

Unit: *broad waking*

The hard season has left
an apricot tree in the window,
the smell of crushed leaves from the riverbank.
It takes so many words to say the sound of water—
a faltering, gated whisper,
the flush of a skirt in the hallway.

Always there will be a dream, always
a waking. Someone will come to stand in the doorway,
or darkness will come to stand in the doorway.
Think of everything in terms of absence:
no snow is falling, nothing held
in the high branches of the tree.

Fever

It comes fully formed, primal,
the smell of skinned pears.
It comes grease-limbed,
through the light-line around the door,
through the seam of the dress
the color of pears. It comes dinnerless
and able, loud in the hold of the throat.
The throat is the stem of the pear,
the sky in the absence of stars.
The throat is my father in his black suit,
come in from the cold. Oh bladeless heart,
who will brush away the snow?
Who will unglove his hands?

Ambulance

I speak as if my voice is a guidewire
sliding toward my brother's heart,
opening each vessel's glossy skin, lighting
the coal stove inside. Warmth might begin
rising upward, his cheeks coloring like twin flowers.
I narrate the roads we drive by memory:
The coastline north of the airport, I say,
the tunnel beneath the harbor, and the city's summer
market, each storefront closed. If I could see
my mother, where she sits beside the driver,
I'd see how tears can look like sweat—
as though she's been running
some long distance, her hair the wiry stems
of orchids in my father's greenhouse.
When I was young, he lifted a caught sparrow
from the soil bed and set it in my hands.
It rolled to its side, clawless, injured
in the falling. *Toss it up,* my father said,
maybe it will fly. The truth is,
I bring my father to the poem only
suddenly, to amend the law of his absence,
and because my brother's eyes are closed.

My Parents Say

Here is what we've given you:
our arms, our stories, our voices
through the floorboards.

Yes, exactly so.

We carried you between us.
When we were working, you crawled
under our desks and slept there,
beside the heels of our shoes.

(I touched the laces.)

Was this not enough?
It was enough.
But you come here to open our marriage, our failing?

Here is the chisel, the axe,
the scroll saw left in the grass.
See how the paper wasps have wakened,
slow from their half-sleep, the chill.

Cradle

After the whitecloud
evidence has been removed
from your lungs, you
bleed in the gauze's spread sail.
All along the highway

lid-lines of turtles
new-hatched in the drainage ditch
blink in shelled moonlight.

The cars dreadlock
into the suburbs, their taillights steadily out-moving
the evening's entering in.

The glandular stink
of eucalyptus, the work-odor
of one who has fought
all night for breath.
Beside your bed, I read by the stars
your hand has penned in the pages' corners.

To think of the end now
is like being nettled to the calves,
each sting a steel sigh.

Any heave from you settles my heart.

The story is one of the unlikely
horse, road-snow
white, two-headed, bound.

It is not for you
when I lift breathing tube and lead wire
to lie beside you.
It is not for you when I hold my mouth
to the cold barrel of your shoulder.

Waiting Room

There were women with wet eyes, women sunning
in the smell and scorch.
There were benches on which no one sat,
though there were people to sit beside—
Around us the city burned. In grief.
In love. It burned
to its knees, leaving its glass
patella, its fibula, its steely heart.
There was a deep voice
which was the door. There was wind
arriving, passing through—
We stood in a forest of high-waisted trees, of starlings.

Ballooning

he wanted to go
he crawled in
his mother folded a cloth
she held his hair between her fingers
shh shh, little one
he sat underneath, looking up
he sat in the box, looking up
he sat in the basement, looking up
but he couldn't see the door
the lightbulb at the top of the stairs
swing swing, little thing
little thing, without a swing
his father cut the rope

close your eyes, little one!
She took up the scissors

Anchors aweigh!

Because he wanted to go up
Because there was a way to crawl in
Because the dome crinkled like tinfoil over a pie plate
Because it crinkled, his hair stood on end
Because the nylon shushed like his mother's skirt
Because the nylon puffed like the school's new parachute
Because there was a box in the basement
Because there was a basement with a very large box
Because there was a bird in his father's stomach
Because inside he was a bird in his father's stomach
Because the backyard swing was broken
Because it was broken, a tire downed in the yard
Because there was rope, but not enough
Because there was an eye in the sky's blue parachute
Because he was growing a wing already
Because he was growing a wing, his knees suffered
Because he could say
Because he could say, *Blast-off!*
Because there was so much space

Children's Story

Dad is throwing a party; he can't stay.

Dad is putting on his winter coat.

Mom is showering because the water's hot.

Dad says, "where there's a will, there's a way."

Dad is putting on his winter hat.

Dad will tap the back of brother's hand before he goes.

Brother is here with his eyes closed.

Brother's eyes are paralyzed.

Brother's eyes won't move even if he dreams.

Dad is making a crown roast for the party.

Brother's breathing has gone mechanical.

Dad has a secret recipe.

Mom is standing in the shower because the water's hot.

Nurse is flushing the lines in the back of brother's left hand.

God has reached his two hands into brother's two lungs and stolen all the air.

Nurse is flushing the lines in the back of brother's right hand.

Brother's two lungs are two empty escape pods.

Nurse is delivering the nighttime paralytic.

Nurse adjusts brother's right leg.

Sister adjusts brother's left leg.

God is a dirty thief.

Nurse feels for fever in the old-fashioned way, by touching the fore-
head.

Missive (1)

Where the river quiets, back turned
to the sun's eyeing, father,
father, take back your baskets of bread.
I have left your long-laid table.
Pour out the milk, father, clear the platters
of dusky fish, the potatoes
and husked corn, the halved
peaches held in two-handed goblets.
Bury the chicken bones where the dogs won't dig
and leave the gristle to the squirrels.

Father, I have kept my swallows small.
They pull and tender against me
where the throat is warm.
I no longer see it is you
standing on the train's platform.

One day, I will no longer remember
the story of my father at the door:
that all day he waited there looking
at the sun and the empty street,
the sun going down and the blue
windows turning their lights out
to the sidewalk in perfect squares,
as if the soles of his feet would print
the threshold in ash, as if I would
come to sweep the doorstep.

Mothering

A mother leaves her son at a Nebraska Hospital under Nebraska's Safe Haven Laws, 2008

It was not as easy as everyone has imagined.
The drive was not silent, rainy, marred
by the hours of his sleeping. We listened
to radio by night, and later to the circling
sprinkler systems clicking over the fields
like great, many-beaked birds. By the time
the time came, the car was emptied.
He moved slowly. I had packed his things.
The rest was accomplished in the idling
air let out by two revolving doors. Quickly:
the only fair way. The freeway, after that,
continued straight through. In another thousand miles,
California, where they say the houses on the cliffs
far north of San Francisco are affordable,
painted the color of shells found on glass shelves
in beach town souvenir shops. They say the fog waits
outside the windows three hundred days a year.

Care

When the intubation tube comes out,
you refuse to swallow. It hurts.
No one can coax you into it.
They sit you up and I'm amazed
at how much the body produces:
saliva runs the corners of your mouth,
leveling in the nest of your collarbone.

On the hospital lawn, tables are set for a fundraiser.
Women circle in the garden, dresses
like shades of bottle glass. The season
for jonquils is over: blooms wash up
on their beds like starfish.

I wipe your mouth.
I wipe the cup of your ear.
I use thirty washcloths. I use the loose ends of the sheet.
I use the sleeve of my shirt, the body of my shirt. My hands and my
    forearms.
In the strong overheads, you gleam.

Somewhere, you are gliding through
all the rooms of your sleeping.
If I could make your eyes open,
I would bring you the window.
See how the cluster flies search out the closeted
places, the wall voids and soffits?
Little curators of darkness
and necessity, overwintering here.

Unit: *little stars were the herring fish*

Then they waited in places that resembled sleep:
an airshaft window slightly open, an up-rise
of yellow air, a dog's closeted barking.

*

They were folded into ordinary flowers,
held in someone's palm a long time and later
pressed until their colors bled into the pages
of a dictionary. They were folded
into small, captainless boats and paper fortune tellers
worked by the fingers—blue: four, green: five—
of a girl, open-mouthed, mouthing

*

love. Then, they loved again.
But without the sturdy steam-engine
conviction of first love, one refused to rise
from bed. Another sipped halfheartedly
at the vein of air shuttled into the room,
lake-blue across the mouth,
fingers white as threads of milk

*

across the window's blue lake. Then, artificial,
worked-for sleep set a hand over the eyes, and the eyes
of sleep were the milky eyes of a mother leaving.

*

Then, one shuffled cards, television stations, coins
from hand to hand. One sat in the closed kitchen,
recipe cards dealt on the floor:
handwritten (by lovers and ex-lovers, mothers
and their mothers) never-baked breads. Egg-white
tiles, true-white walls. A cold oven.

Escape

I know how to tell it: C is for Cat   D for Dead   E
for Elephant, Escape. Or Esplanade where news channel 10 tells us
the zoo's lost leopard was last sighted

       You think you see it   where the boats are going
out on the river

       Little brother   your skin is too fragile for scratching!
                                              Your cheeks are already bleeding!
The aspirator sucks out your spit   snakes it
to the biohazard   body-fluid-
                                     bin behind the bed

       When the squads arrive
                                     the antechamber hissing
                                     sterilization   sanitation
                                     desensitization-by-sound
they have the quiet feet of elephants padding around
                                     in their contamination suits

their gray   monolithic thighs their bellies and broad breasts

                                     their needling

careful trunks   Careful!   They change
your bloody sheets   your shit-on sheets
the vomity slick of your sheets   They roll you
left shoulder
                                   to right shoulder
They touch you with the razor tips of their tusks

       Little brother   B is for you
                                   bird in the sight of someone's rifle
                                   beloved unburiable body

there is no food you can swallow
there is no sleep for you
the sky is very blue

the glass sealed shut

Little brother
the boats are going out on the river
There are reports that a leopard has escaped
and tomorrow it will be sunny

Don't end with the weather
you say

Say you see it

Family Portrait: ICU

The roof dances until it is quiet.
We sit still
as if we had unlearned the logic
of logic.
In the museum of the wished-for:
woman as chestnut tree, man
with a wing—
wing with a peony of lead
hung in the feathers.

He takes the feeding tube:
music after only a minute.
When he moves a little, excited—excited
she sounds like water.
And the disadvantage of parting:
we must
unlearn the name of each town
in which we paused—
Jaw Lapse, Sand Spit,
Unfired Forge.

2

C&O

A train runs south along river
and state-line, each mountain
turning down to each dusky window.

We are briefly double-lit:
streetlight, moon felled in a darkening
western field. All night

you shook: your sleep
nearly breaking: I stilled
your body against me. Against the updraft,

a nuthatch closed in the tree's
airy warehouse, wings softened
and built for winter

(hawks commit their circles
over the grassy limit of the road
looking for the animal)

lake country impossible to leave.

Sunday Morning with Music

Sometimes winding along the sky-register,
sometimes dreamed as turning

through water, mud, the periglacial
lake reeds—though whatever noise they make

is haphazard, all bristling mane
and the horse itself,

or lovers returning
from wherever the fire was to wherever

the body is, cold.
Percussives, we rattle

against each other toward the wire outskirt
of what the eye can see:

the boat hauled out of the water,
the rower's torso lean as the hull

as he lifts from shadow
into shadow until the whole grooved network,

rower and scull, is inseparable,
sturdy and tipped blue.

Poem for the Beloved's Lover

He holds you all night, other pale other, the ether
netted over the attic bed. Eucalyptus, tinder, an acre
of sedge, this window I also will wake under.

Three

:what we entered into faithfully,

as the moon's strict route, as the green's insistence on the trees.

We believed in ourselves this capacity.

But no water was brought to the coughing one, no pill to the sleepless.

If there is only one hour to mourn, which hour?

The Outer Banks

1

Orion rose in its sculpted circle,
slow as a house-fly surfacing to a lamp.

Moonless. Nothing to shadow
the dune's pelvic indent, no shine

on the tips of the grasses. The sky's purse turned
over on our small table,

the stars loosed in their high room, windows
skittering in the upper register of a house.

2

The only writing surface was the palm of the hand,
where the flesh's slight give mistook our words.

Love held again its old solitude,
a far harbor entered

through parallel breakwaters:
the long voice, the mouth in smoke.

3

The camera's shutter would not forgive us
our tremble, and in the safelight

you come back to me sweating,
a gray shore in the stop-bath's standing water.

Widow's Walk

The first mate swabs the deck
with spit the second mate is wife

For years you inked your calling
on the longboard of my back

The sea back then was so like me
for years she called you home

Montolieu

1

From his high seat, the driver leans out the window,
holds his palm to the wall of the town,
gauging what space he has. His sleeve
opens along the sill of his arm, fingers
gentling over the shallow doorway the way he must
touch his wife's shirt in the mornings
as she stands beside him washing dishes,
glasses given to him to dry,
brim, seam and the leftover soap
caught in the hollow. All is ordered by this:
her hands to his, the dishtowel passing between them.

2

The afternoon stretches, white
sheets on a clothesline
full with their own flat sound.
The storm has turned back.
You pour milk in the cradle of coffee,
sugar the mouth of the spoon.
Without a look, you crush your cigarette.
Without a look: stir.
If the heart has a thousand windows
I will close them.

3

This is how the river sounds through the windows.
They will not open. The glass is recognized as glass
only when it shakes in the sills.
The noise is like coughing at night.
The noise, like stacking dishes in the sink.

The river concedes nothing. Each tulip
along the house tightens nightly:
a child who waits for his skinned knee to bleed,
the scrape losing its color, suddenly
almost white. The river offers
its protection, funnels light
to hallways too small to walk through.

4

The Virgin: one woman
in a field of men who pale
on their crosses.
Their failed bodies,
fruit falling.
Evening comes in a sudden stop.
Stars, more forward,
give up their darknesses,
envy the small
gesture of her arms.
A closed cup,
the night's flower,
all her shine thrown inward.

5

You have left a bowl of cherries
on the table: they chafe
against each other, skins opening
their small theaters of color,
the red in the garden
that pricks the fingers.
The ceiling creases in light,
a handkerchief folding open.
These cherries: so much trouble,
so little sweetness in the mouth.

Figurehead

Because the book is dedicated to no one,
I began to travel by steamer—

each departed beach bestial,
and blue's newest episode.

When I heard my sound separate from yours,
a sinew raw-scraped, blood-twined between the fingers,

sugarwater filled my yearling mouth,
still-barned, slow, yet so like the salty,

open-hatched wail of *wife* or *fuse* or *home*.
It is not that I do not love you,

beached in clay and masted potato vine,
its anchored root in place of me.

Dido's Dream

1

Love sent its patrols city to city,
house to house, house
on the edge of the water, bent late
in the late storm. The high-water line bent
inland, full of weed and shell, of women
bent down, covering their heads,

2

their names written beside each other in a register, in cold ink:

3

Desire, Prayer, Fire—
—late, last in the mouth,
eyes closed with two flowered coins,
flowers into bulbs, full-grown trees into saplings.

4

Warmth to bring the bees from the paralytic sleep—a consciousness
waking slow in the unwakable muscle—from the hive
where they have cleaned and closed the entrances,
a thousand steadfast husbands.

5

One by one, things turn to stone.
Each ankle. Each knee. The bees in the window. Each bracelet
dropped from the wrist. Twelve white stones turn stone on the floor.

6

The bed burns. Someone says,
Lie down on the ground, as you've been taught, to avoid the smoke,
to avoid

7

first: wings: sound.
Two beats a beating
against the neck.
The hair is cut black
hair peeled away
sky thin as a wing.

If

If this love had lasted, there would have been a child.
But in a day even this wanting is lifted
in the automatic double set of double doors,

two quick breaths, shallow, unconcerned
with the diaphragm, and a woman's hands open
in explanation or sorrow. The night resolves

in the clicks of a thousand imagined cicadas.
I sleep again in my mother's house.
On the snow's white sheet, the moon comes back doubled.

Afterlove

A thousand ships to get here,
I sent messengers to plead with you

across an ocean

I sent desire. When nothing returned
I sent the pale-handed
harbinger of war.

You faltered.
Hope's stiff carriers crowded
my rooms, an army
of competing clatter
and rust.

In the leftover
quiet
wind too slight to lift the hair from my neck,

I saw there was something still
for each of us to want.

Gulls dispersed, white
above the roofline, so white
I could not tell
one from the other, nor one
from the sky.

Letters from Morocco

Marrakech

The light goes on,
goes off in the courtyard
below the window.
Someone is walking
in a long coat. Someone is
loved beyond reason,
someone not at all.
Somewhere there is a beach,
a moon rising in every stone eye.
I dream of rice paper
and a closet of pressed clothes.
I must intend to stay
all night writing this letter
to you, familiar, unbeloved.

Essaouira

I lie all night
in Élouard's fiberglass apse.
La mer n'a plus de lumière
et, comme aux temps anciens,
ask me to return to our bed,
or instead come to the dock
fearless, handkerchiefless,
waving to no one.

Chefchaouen

It has been quiet
among the clay and the wire
hairline streets.
The mosque is lit
all night though the fountain stops.
No one says why.
The valley is filled with ornamental trees
turning flower instead of fruit.
The valley is further than it seems.

In a Familiar City

where the grass and the gravel tic-tic-tic
on the pavement, the morning
sprinters, or on the mountain
where there are no trees, or just one,
grown light and thinned out of the rock:
there might as well be music.
There might as well be a certain resting
sky, and a picnic to which we are invited.
There is plenty of room.
The flowerboxes are full of ice. At home,

where the loss has always already happened,
and the birds have only just come back,
the trouble and clench of your fingers
are irretrievable in the room's
studio-bright light. There are onlookers:
white dress left over a door. Day-moon,
hole in the sky's blue body-armor.
How small the road seems
in comparison, the lean starts
of redbuds spiked up the drive.

Hotel

There is the semblance of being cared for
in the white, made-up bed,
and in the women on the balconies
repairing the hems of their dresses.
Questions may be directed
to the man behind the desk;
a line has already formed.
When I arrive at dinner, I am expected
alone at the table beside the window.
There is no need for the pretense of books.
Snow slips the roof so easily
you can imagine what it is like
to have never loved. It was enough
for these things—bread and silver,
winter trees in the ice field—
to be held effortlessly, casually
as an armful of flowers.

3

Owl

So named for her waking nights
for the eyes that dream drove open
to the serrated plane of roof-beamed-by-river.

So named by the always-morning-
faced nurses she saw cellared in her fingertip-
counting: screws and dowels

holding headboard to needled-out nocturne:
bed-rail rapped by nail,
glass under rain, paid-for

by the weatherman's false call, and the fair-weather
never-in-snow approach by overnight train
of a whistle half-aired,

half unroused in the pipe. So named for an inability
to wake with the others.
For the obvious rhyme.

For the slipped hunter, the sharp-edged use of the trowel,
and because she could see what was coming.
Even at night she could see

the factory's horizoning plumage,
an outbuilding abbreviated by landslide,
its howl hung lengthwise from the last rafter.

Unit: *woods these are*

Single bed, single
window. The sky
a blue lamp. He is
bending over the hallway
of her legs, his hand
a terse knuckled cup.
How else to be familiar
with the cold newly arrived,
the hayfield split dry
under tractor wheels?
The distance to the window
is one she can measure.
Four steps, maybe. A slip
of light. He looks
happy. She doesn't know
where to pose her lips.

Vecuronium Bromide

locked in the lights turned out
at the end of a long room a small bed
hail breaks the gable window   a shock!
the foghorn loudsounds
                   a loudmouth
in the nursery   a true doll
in her smocked dress pleases everyone
the curtains full of water
                 water
fills a mixing bowl   beneath the gable a bed
everyone pleases   with her mouth
with her true hips   the full wet curtain
with her hornsound
               a singsong
in the gable   a small bed
a glass breaking at the end of the room
the lights' longsong turned out
                  turns out
her toes   the barre is the wet windowsill
the footboard of the bed   she makes
a longhouse of her chest   she makes
a foghorn of her mouth   she pliés
                    practices
from her hips a nurserysong
a mouth a lockturn a breaking glass
she pliés   she practices   the shock   it's true
                      pleases everyone

Lorazepam

Quick, sweet, restless:
the afternoon sex that allows sleep

until dinner, dinner
dressed and candled, an unlit

hall walked to the table,
to the spiced and substantial,

the inhale of tamarind
and fennel seed,

a heaviness set in the spine's
cellar, the stomach's

moony table kissed by many
mouths, mouthed by many hands;

stopping, stopping, the sleeping's
stony anaphora.

Deborah Digges is Dead

The vein was never opened by the needle's little head; the carbon
dioxide did not ratchet up any debt in the blood.
No part was shaved.
The stomach was not plumed by syringe, nor was there tubing for
urine, for spit.
The pulse was well contained in the bed of the neck: with the naked
eye, no one could detect it.
The sun did not come up in rooms walked by those who each day
heard the birds' first call.
The blankets remained cool, the skin not sweated, nor marked by
unchanged linen.
A gown was never tied about the shoulders.
There were no visitors. No vase of circus roses. No water poured
from the pitcher, nor ice given on the worst nights, in the usual
way of things.

Nevertheless, a teacup slipped its hook.
It was not meant to be painless.
In the sink, a regular shattering, though it was not without
the sound of barking dogs. And still the water boiled.
All it meant was that a woman had opened a window from her
fitted sleep
as we stood watching a crow take to the air haphazardly, just-then
sprung from well below the earth.

Unit: *it would be life*

Pink out
the pinnate window

above my pin-hole
eating table –

the house across lights
its top-floor pinnace

portholes – a crownrow
of rounds

for the downstairs
salon with Pioneer

sofa and plushless anchor
rug, the upright piano

washed in alluvial orange
from the doorless kitchen door.

I have never seen a family there.
But beneath a chandelier

of repro addax
horns; beneath a partners' desk

with neither chair; and
though it sounds untrue:

a stone bowl's acitabulum
fit to a child's skull

is filled with yellow flowers –
pimpernel or pseudo?

In winter they'll be blue.

Puppetry

Elephant, with paper trunk.
Hold an open book
across the bridge of the nose:
bird with a coverboard beak.
For adornment: a quartz
spur on a copper chain.
Decoration aside,
men of genius suffer
breakdowns, men of faith
lie together on the stadium floor.
A god's feckless beak
snaps on the stall's wall
shadowcast by my kinking
hands. Hold open for me
the book that illustrates
the bridge a longspur makes,
tree to chain to feeder,
to nose the easy seeds free.
Fold for me that paper
elephant who without
decoration, sigh or cover
of night, inters her dead
love with her trunk,
with her blunt elephant feet.

Haberdashery

Notice the clingy stink
of sea things pinned on sand.
A smell particularly
Atlantic, one unnoticed
by one like me: born here.
When they've ticked your name
off the passenger list, and you
are asked, professionally,
to board, your voice's downy
afterfeather is the first to go
in the clippings of wings, the horn,
the island fog. The fog
goes north a hundred clicks,
the captain, and you, go north.
Professionally, he checks
the compass now and then.
The gulls drop girlish
afterfeathers on the deck.
On the dock I tick your name
on the pads of my fingers.
Darling, the Atlantic will burn
your hands. Something clings
to the side of the boat.
The stink pins me to your collar.

Vinalhaven Island

1

The bulb of the ocean,
clam-rich, shoe-swallowing.
If you live here, you find a skiff that can make the crossing.

Safe-house, water-palace.
Small rivers the slippers
step over. Plaster-work, mosaic, a sailor's alphabet

on the wall. First salt: mud
tasted in the arm's crease,
in the black around the nostrils. Even the fog won't shade

the light, it will only
disperse it. When is it
no longer the season to remember those lost to us?

At night I touch your back
as my mother touched mine.
Cow-slow, you move off into sleep. For years I have been caught

rowing home too late on an empty sea, a changeless tide.

2

At night I touch your back
and sing the sailor's song:

For *C*, the cormorant's
crossing and the clammer's
coveralls dried in sun.

L for the leap of faith
that each one of us takes
when coming this far out.

M, the magnificent
claw-foot tub. The mosaic
mermaid's showy sweeping

S: the skiff's slight safe-house,

and the water-palace
you enter it through. *O*

is the ocean you lick
from the back of my hand.

3

There is no way to know whose arms greeted you, simply that
they must have been there: guards
against rock or pavement,

porcelain claw-foot or the underwater pressure felt
in the ears through too-fast
an ascent—skiff-eating

ocean (safe-house, water-palace) lost last from the nostrils.
There is no way to know
which man was the first to

carve the sailor's first alphabet in the mud we're clamming
in coveralls, licking
the salt from our elbows.

This is not the time to think of those who were lost to us.
Fog magnifies the light.
At night I touch your back as my mother (*mother!*) touched mine.

The Curiosities

I don't believe in poetry. This might be the last poem.

The neighbor's Pekinese barks his little head off
every time I unlock the door. The lock is loose, I can turn it

with a knife. I raise African violets
like those my father used to bring me:
stereoscopic purple, four yellow fish-eyes to a flower.

They make my window
my childhood window.
There were three steeples,
and on the rooftop opposite, a wooden owl.
The seagulls never failed to be fooled.

The mourning doves in the gable woke me up, woke me up, woke
      me up.
I grew up and behind me my brother grew up.

"Bye-bye," I told my father.

I've been living away
on this other coast:
Mexican grackles, saguaros in the south, it snows in the mountains,
bike paths, pie cutter, sex. So many curiosities!
A bridge built to withstand earthquakes.
Earthquakes. Pencil sharpener
in a pool of wooden flakes.

My father has La Caja China ready in his yard.
A grown man could lie inside.
I hear he has shaved off his beard, which I hear
had turned entirely gray.

Because I give those flowers too much
or too little water, my lover cares for them.

When I speak to my mother, I see her in my childhood
house. In my mother's house,
here we are at Christmas.

Once I saw my father's two taupe rooms
at the Extended Stay America in a hitch of the highway's suburban
    loop.
This was no place to live, on the highway's suburban loop.
This was all a long time ago.

Any passerby can see me with my violets:
There is no privacy.

I keep my hair clean, and long. It ties itself up without a pin.
They say my father has a lovely house and tomatoes trellised up the
    porch.
But the intelligence is old.

Any passerby can see the ultraviolet blue, the little yellow eyes.

The power plant trilled white smoke from its one thin lung.
See it from the playroom window.
I chewed until polish came off in my teeth.

My father is preparing La Caja China for a hog.
His butcher has split the rib cage and laid the halves flat.

My mother held my head in her lap.
My lover holds my feet in his hands.

My brother and I listened from the breakwater.
From the Willows we heard the sirens
of Skee-Ball machines spitting out their hundred tickets,
GRAND PRIZE, when the wind was right.
For a hundred tickets: a plastic kaleidoscope, pencil
sharpener shaped as goldfish,
pirate's eye patch.

My father loads the box with coals.

Here September is the hottest month.
The flies dress the apples up in black lace.
There is no lung-fill green.

My father injects the mojo beneath the skin with a marinade syringe.
When he is very afraid, and though we are mostly grown up,

my brother asks me to lie beside him.

Father, you were right
when you said I am different now: I am different now.
Tonight you will feed your forty friends.

Missive (2)

I don't believe in beauty: my lover

beside me
        beautiful: my father often

a liar: I don't believe

you: my father always

I love you: father
        I am always saying

father: you have never been

here in this house:
        mother beside her lover

sleeping, brother and his often-lover

       radiator hiss or is it whisper?

asleep in the room next door.

Here as in everywhere: father

I am always calling you. Here

it is Christmas Eve: I don't believe:

       lights-in-snow:

Actually snowing.

Plowing

It's a loud business, to the untrained
ear. And so much snow, it's hard to imagine
a road ever existed here. Even the truck,
tire-chained, back-weighted by a full bed of sand,
can't hold its corners, entering the sliplace
of crusted pasture, even once disarraying
someone's spring-stacked heap of burn wood.
And as the plow's grunt dislodges
a buried walkway's in-ground light,
we're pitched so hard against the dash
my watch's crown cuts in my wrist a perfect hole.
My brother in his undershirt climbs through the window
to dig wheel from bank with a small shovel.
When he holds his sustained weight
against the bumper, I'm to turn the wheel,
clutch, give a little gas. Those of us who wait
for the quiet after the storm, may wait.

Acknowledgments

I am grateful to the editors of the following publications, in which these poems (sometimes in earlier drafts or with different titles) first appeared: *Anderbo.com*, "Letters from Morocco;" *The Bellevue Literary Review*, "Unit: *broad waking*;" *Blood Orange Review*, "Hotel," "Poem for the Beloved's Lover," "Three;" *Connotation Press*, "Deborah Digges is Dead," "The Curiosities," "Montolieu;" *Diner*, "Unit: *little stars were the herring fish*;" *Drunken Boat*, "Fever," "Figurehead," "Sunday Morning with Music;" *Linebreak*, "Missive (2);" *Lo-Ball*, "Haberdashery," "Owl;" *Southern Poetry Review*, "Plowing;" *Swink Magazine*, "Dido's Dream," "Puppetry," "Vinalhaven Island;" *The The Poetry Blog*, "In a Familiar City;" *TriQuarterly*, "Afterlove," "Escape," "Father."

I would like to thank the Creative Writing Programs at Stanford University and at the University of Virginia for the fellowship support that allowed me time to write. To my teachers, who gave my work their full attention, I am most grateful, particularly to Eavan Boland, Deborah Digges, Deborah Eisenberg, Ken Fields, Charlotte Gordon, Barbara Helfgott Hyett, Lisa Russ Spaar, and Charles Wright. Thanks to Kim Addonizio, Jennifer Foerster, Keetje Kuipers, Randy Mann, Doug Powell, and Matthew Siegel: my San Francisco. Finally, to Leigh Perham, who showed me the way, and to Peter Kline, who went with me: thank you. With you I am home.

About the Author

Brittany Perham is a Jones Lecturer in Poetry at Stanford University, where she was a Wallace Stegner Fellow from 2009-2011. Her work may be found in the *Bellevue Literary Review, Drunken Boat, Lo-Ball, Southern Poetry Review, TriQuarterly*, and elsewhere. She lives in San Francisco.

Photograph of the author by Nike Perlet. Used by permission.

Free Verse Editions

Edited by Jon Thompson

13 ways of happily by Emily Carr
Between the Twilight and the Sky by Jennie Neighbors
Blood Orbits by Ger Killeen
The Bodies by Chris Sindt
Child in the Road by Cindy Savett
Country Album by James Capozzi
The Curiosities by Brittany Perham
Current by Lisa Fishman
Divination Machine by F. Daniel Rzicznek
The Flying House by Dawn-Michelle Baude
Instances: Selected Poems by Jeongrye Choi, translated by Brenda
    Hillman, Wayne de Fremery, and Jeongrye Choi
A Map of Faring by Peter Riley
Physis by Nicolas Pesque, translated by Cole Swensen
Poems from above the Hill & Selected Work by Ashur Etwebi, trans-
    lated by Brenda Hillman and Diallah Haidar
The Prison Poems by Miguel Hernández, translated by Michael Smith
Puppet Wardrobe by Daniel Tiffany
Quarry by Carolyn Guinzio
remanence by Boyer Rickel
Signs Following by Ger Killeen
These Beautiful Limits by Thomas Lisk
An Unchanging Blue: Selected Poems 1962–1975 by Rolf Dieter
    Brinkmann, translated by Mark Terrill
Under the Quick by Molly Bendall
Verge by Morgan Lucas Schuldt
The Wash by Adam Clay
We'll See by George Godeau, translated by Kathleen McGookey
What Stillness Illuminated by Yermiyahu Ahron Taub
Winter Journey [Viaggio d'inverno] by Attilio Bertolucci, translated
    by Nicholas Benson

www.ingramcontent.com/pod-product-compliance
Lightning Source LLC
Chambersburg PA
CBHW032030090426
42741CB00006B/796